Dictionary of
Roman Military Terms

Frank Graham

First published by Frank Graham
Published by Butler Publishing in 1989
This reprint 2000

©1989
ISBN 0946928347

Butler Publishing
Thropton, Morpeth
Northumberland NE65 7LP

BUTLER
publishing

The following dictionary of Roman military terms contains almost 300 words and covers most of those in general use. The main source has been *A Latin Dictionary* by Lewis and Short, 1927. *The Roman Imperial Army* by Graham Webster, 1969, has been of great help. Russell Robinson's two books - *What the Soldiers Wore on Hadrian's Wall*, 1976, and *The Armour of the Roman Legions*, 1980, have been quoted on numerous occasions. *The Roman Army* by Peter Connolly has also been used.

In most cases we have given only the singular form of the words.

Romans taking prisoners

ACCENSI   Reserve troops who followed the army as supernumeraries to take the place of those who fell in battle.

ACIES   Line of battle.

ACTUARIUS   Clerk who kept accounts.

ADIUTOR   A common name of a military officer. Adjutant.

AERARIUM MILITARE   Military treasury.

AGGER   Rampart. A mound of earth used in defence works.

AGMEN   The marching column.

AGRIMENSOR   A surveyor. See *metatores*.

ALA   Cavalry regiment.

AMBULATURAE   Field manoeuvres.

ANNONA MILITARIS   Annual military tax. A tax in kind (corn) from the province which the Wall defended.

AQUILA   Eagle standard which was carried by each legion. During the Empire it was made of gold. See *Vexillum*.

AQUILIFER   Senior standard bearer, the one who carried the eagle.

ARCHITECTUS   Architect or builder. The fine altar at Birrens to the goddess Brigantia was set up by an architect called Amandus.

AREANI   Frontier scouts who operated north of the Wall. They were disbanded in 368.

ARMILLA   Arm band. A military decoration.

AUGUR   A priest who examines natural happenings to see if they are propitious.

AULOS   A pipe with a shrill note used at sacrifices to drown any noise.

AUXILIARIES   Soldiers other than legionaries.

BALLISTA   A military machine to throw projectiles. Originally it was different from the *Catapulta* which was used for throwing arrows, but afterwards interchanged with it.

BALLISTARIUM   A catapult-platform as can be seen at High Rochester.

BALNEUM   Bath house. The plan of Chesters bath house gives the Roman names of the various rooms.

BALTEUS   Baldric. A sword belt passing over the shoulder.

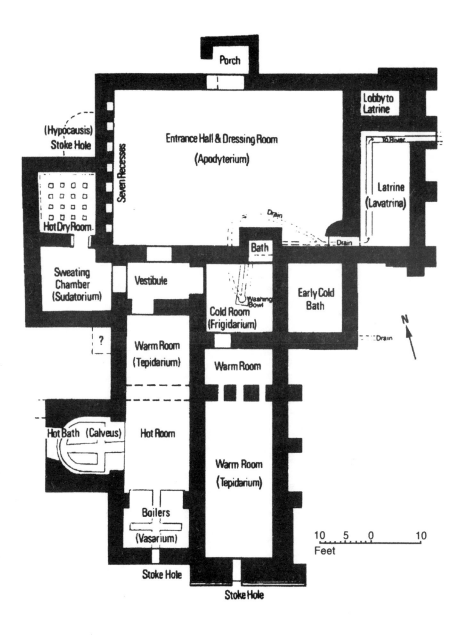

Bath house at Chesters Fort (on the Roman Wall)

5

BASILICA EQUESTRIS EXERCITATORIA   A cavalry drill-hall. The Roman name is recorded in an inscription at Netherby. Little is known of these halls in Britain. At Haltonchesters one was built during the Severan reconstruction.

BASILICA EXERCITATORIA   A drill-hall.

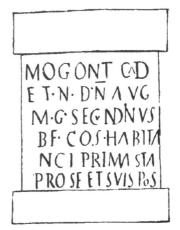

Deo Mogonti Cadenorum et Numini Domini noftri Augufti Marcus Gaius Secundinus beneficiarius confulis Habitanci prima ftatione pro fe et fuis pofuit

BENEFICIARIUS   Soldiers who, through the favour of their commanders, were exempt from menial services such as throwing up entrenchments and foraging. They were the orderlies, or rather aides, or senior officers. In the late 2nd century we find the *beneficiarius* used as a custom officer. There was one at Housesteads. At Risingham an altar to Mogons was erected by a *beneficarius consularis*.

BIPENNIS   Double-bladed axe.

BIREME   A galley with two bands or oars.

BRACAE   Trousers or breeches originally worn by barbarians. Later, in cold climates, the legionaries were allowed to wear *bracae* of leather. They were skin tights and reached below the knees.

Watch-tower on the Roman Wall

BUCCELLATA   Soldiers' biscuits. Corn-meal baked hard and used when on campaigns.

BUCINA   A crooked horn or trumpet (the *tuba* is usually straight). It was used for ceremonial occasions and for regulating the watches. *Ad primam bucinam*, at the first watch, *Ad secundam bucinam*, at the second watch. The men who blew them were called *bucinatores*.

BURGUS   Watch-tower.

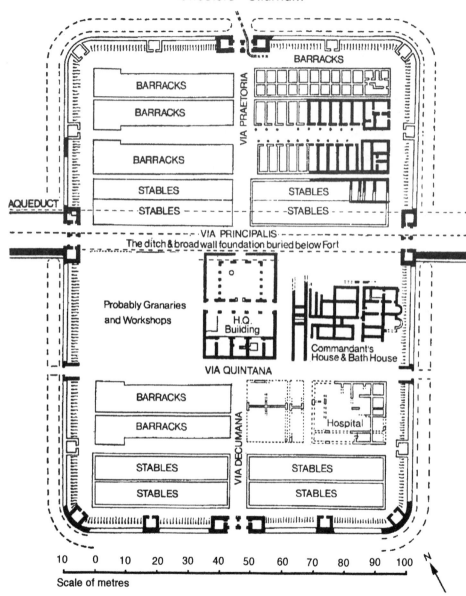

A fort on the Roman Wall

CAETRA   A short Spanish shield.

CAETRATI   Troops armed with the *caetra*.

CALIGA   A military shoe or boot.

CALO   A servant (usually a slave) acting as a batman for the legionaries.

CANABA   A hovel or hut, a "booth". Name used for a civilian settlement round a legionary fortress. The people were called *canabenses*.

CAPSARIUS   Medical orderly. He was a dresser or bandager who carried a round box of bandages (*capsa*) in the field. Also used for a slave who took care of the clothes in the baths.

CARCER   Prison. No example in Britain.

CARROBALLISTA   A ballista mounted on a carriage.

CASSIS   A helmet. See *galea*.

CASTRUM   Roman fort.

CATAPHRACTUS   Armoured cavalryman. *Cataphracts* or fully armoured horsemen were used in the Roman Army in the time of Hadrian. His Governor of Cappadocia in A.D. 137, in his famous work on tactics, wrote: "in the armoured cavalry (*cataphraetarii) b*oth horse and man are protected, the horses onthe sides and front, the rider with body-armour of mail and thigh guards". For a fine reconstruction of a *cataphractus* see *The Armour of the Roman Legions,* by H. Russell Robinson, 1980.

CATAPULTA   Arrow-shooting machine.

CATTUS   Moveable shed as protection for besiegers (also called *pluteus or vinea).*

CENA   Dinner in evening. One of the two meals in the army, see *Prandium.*

CENTURIA   Century. A unit of 80 men.

CENTENARII   Early name for centurion.

CERARIUS   A clerk. One who wrote on wax *(cera)*.

CERVUS   A chevaux-de-frise. A quick-set thorn hedge was often used on a slope for defence.

CINGULUM   Belt.

CINGULUM MILITARE   Military belt.

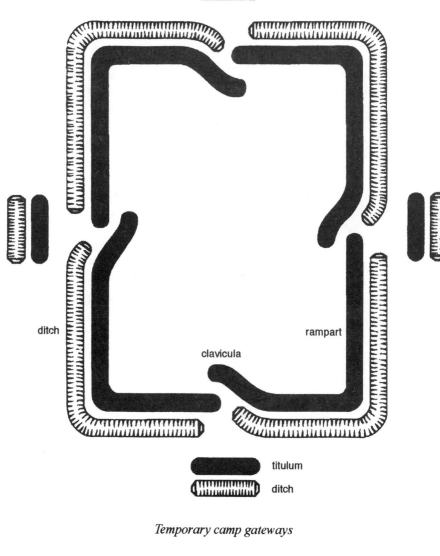

ditch

rampart

clavicula

titulum

ditch

Temporary camp gateways

10

CIPPUS   A wooden stake used as a boundary mark or sharpened to form a protective wall.

CLASSICUM   A fanfare. Battle signal upon the trumpet.

CLAVICULA   Method of defending a gate by a ditch which swung outwards in a curve. See *titulum*.

CLIBANARIUS   A soldier clad in mail. See *cataphractarii*.

CLIBANUS   Small oven for baking bread.

CLIPEUS   A round shield.

COHORS   Cohort. An infantry unit normally consisting of either ten (*miliaria*) or five (*quingenaria*) centuries of eighty men.

COHORS EQUITATA   These units of five-hundred or a thousand men were part infantry and part cavalry.

COLUMBARIA   A tomb with many niches.

COMES   Count. The title was created by Constantine *cf. comes litoris Saxonici*.

COMITATENSES   Field armies as opposed to frontier troops.

CONTARII   A type of cavalry who were armed in the normal manner but carried the long *contus*, "the lance used by the Persians, Parthian and Sarmatian heavy cavalry. The only representation of Roman *contarii* is on the Trajan Column where they are shown in undress uniform standing in a group holding their horses with their great lances held vertically. Because the stirrup had not been invented the effect of such a lance as a shock weapon was extremely limited." H. Russell Robinson.

CONTUS   A lance or pike.

CONUBIUM   When discharge from the army a Roman soldier was given Roman citizenship and *conubium*, which was the right to marry and raise Roman citizens.

CORNICEN   A horn blower.

CORNICULARIUS   A secretary or adjutant of a centurion, tribune, etc.

CORNU   A large curved horn. Associated with the standards.

CORONA   A crown. Military decoration.

During the Republic military decorations were won on merit regardless of rank.

The most prized was the siege crown *corona absidionalis* given for the rescue of a besieged army. It was made of grass.

The *corona civica* of oak leaves was awarded to a soldier who saved the life of a fellow citizen

The *corona muralis* in gold was awarded to the first man over the enemy's wall during a siege and the *corona vallaris*, likewise in gold, to the first man over the rampart during a siege.

The *corona navalis* was awarded for the capture of an enemy ship. It could only be worn by a consul.

During the Empire decorations were restricted to certain ranks and a simple gold crown *(corona aurea)* was awarded to centurions and higher ranks.

CORVUS   A boarding bridge. A naval term.

CRISTA   The crest of a helmet.

CRISTA TRANSVERSA   Crest of a centurion which was worn in a transverse position and ornamented with silver so that they could be easily distinguished.

CUCULLUS   Hooded cloak worn by auxiliaries in cold weather.

CUNEUS   Unit of irregular cavalry. See *numerus*.

CURATOR VETERANORUM   Men in a legion who were serving after retiring age were in a separate unit under their own commander *(curator)*.

CUSTOS ARMORUM   Armourer.

DECURIO   A cavalry officer.

DEPOSITA   Soldiers' savings bank.

DIPLOMA   A certificate of Roman citizenship.

DOLABRUM   Axe, or rather pick-axe. At one end was a cutting edge, at the other a tine or projecting point.

DRACO   A standard in the form of a dragon.

DRACONARIUS   A standard bearer. He carried what is known as a dragon standard which was a streamer which wriggled in the breeze like the tail of a dragon.

DUPLICARIUS   Troop commander. A soldier who receives double pay as a reward.

Corona obsidionalis

Corona vallaris

Corona civica

Corona navalis

Corona muralis

Corona aurea

DUX   Duke. The *Notitia Dignitatum* records that the *Dux Britanniarum* commanded the troops on the Roman Wall.
EQUES, EQUITES   Horseman, pl. cavalry.
EQUITES SINGULARES   Governor's bodyguard.

EXACTOR   Tax collector.

EXACTUS   Clerk

EXOSTRA   A hanging bridge, applied by besiegers to the walls of a besieged city.

EXPLORATOR   A scout.

FABRICA   A workshop.

FABRICENSES   Armourers.

FALCES MURALIS   Hooks on long poles with which to pull down walls.

FASTIGATA   A V-shaped ditch.

FOEDERATI   The first settlement of *foederati* in Britain was in 417. They were tribes within the frontier allied with Rome.

Collecting tribute at Carvoran (near the Roman Wall)

14

Soldier with his carrying pole

FORUM Market place.

FOSSA Ditch.

FOSSATUM A flat-bottomed ditch.

FRAMEA A spear or javelin used by the Germans.

FRUMENTARIUS Intelligence officer.

FRUMENTUM Army food supply.

FURCA Carrying pole on which the Roman soldier carried his equipment.

FUSTUARIUM Cudgelling to death, a military punishment for desertion or other capital offences.

GAESUM Large Celtic javelin. There was a vexillation or detachment of men so armed at Greatchesters - *Vexillatio gaesatorum Raetorum.*

GALEA Helmet.

GENIUS Guardian spirit.

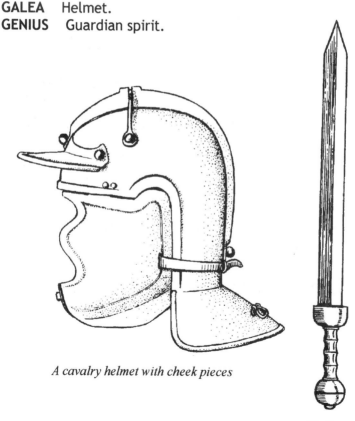

A cavalry helmet with cheek pieces

Gladius

16

Roman granary

GLADIUS   A sword.

GLADIUS HISPANIENSIS   The legionary's sword.

GLANS   An acorn. A ball of lead or clay of acorn-shape used in a sling.

GRAFFITO, GRAFFITI   Picture scratched on stone.

GROMA   Surveying instrument.

HARUSPICES   Priests who practised divination by reading the entrails of sacrificial victims.

HASTA   Spear.

HASTATUS   The front rank of the legion.

HASTA PURA   Small silver spears awarded to legionary commanders and tribunes for distinguished service.

HIBERNA   Winter camp.

HIPPICA GYMNASIA   Cavalry display.

HORREUM   Granary.

HYPOCAUSIS   A furnace supplying hot air to under floor central heating.

IMAGINIFER   A standard bearer.

IMAGO   A standard. It carried a portrait of the Emperor.

IMMUNTIAS   Exemption from fatigues. The men who enjoyed it were *immunes*.

The hypocaust at Binchester (Co. Durham)

IMPEDIMENTA   Heavy baggage carried by the baggage train.
INSIGNIA   A standard.
INTERPRETES   Interpreters.
LAMELLA   Plate of metal, used in armour.
LARARIUM   Household shrine where the *lares* or household
  gods were worshipped.
LAVATRINA   Latrine.
LEGATUS LEGIONIS   Legionary commander.
LEGIO   Roman legion.
LEGIONARIUS   A legionary.
LIBRARIUS   A clerk. Many has special duties: the *librarius
  horreorum* kept the granary records, the *librarius
  depositorum* collected the soldiers' savings, and there was
  even a *librarius caducorum* who looked after the
  belongings of those who were killed in battle.
LICTOR   A bodyguard to the consul.
LIMITANEI   Frontier troops.

LORICA   Breastwork on a rampart. Also means body armour.
LORICA HAMATA   Mail armour.
LORICA SQUAMATA   Scale armour.
LORICA SEGMENTATA   Body armour made of metal strips.
LUDUS LATRUNCULORUM   A game played on a board like
   chess. Popular with the army. Several of these boards have
   been found on the Roman Wall.
MANIPULUS   A *maniple* was a division of a legion, the third
   of a cohort and made up of two centuries.
MANSIO   Inn. Found at Benwell, Corbridge and Vindolanda.

A Roman board-game

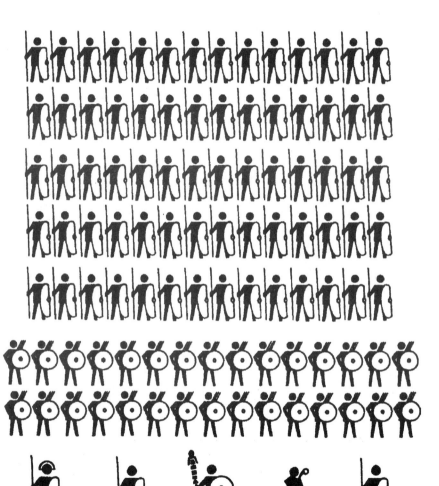

Elected centurion   Optio   Signifer   Cornicen   Tesserarius

HASTATI or PRINCIPES
heavily armed spearmen and 60 velites

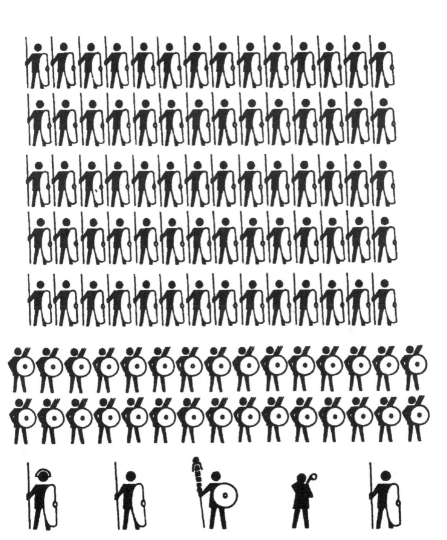

| Nominated centurion | Optio | Signifer | Cornicen | Tesserarius |

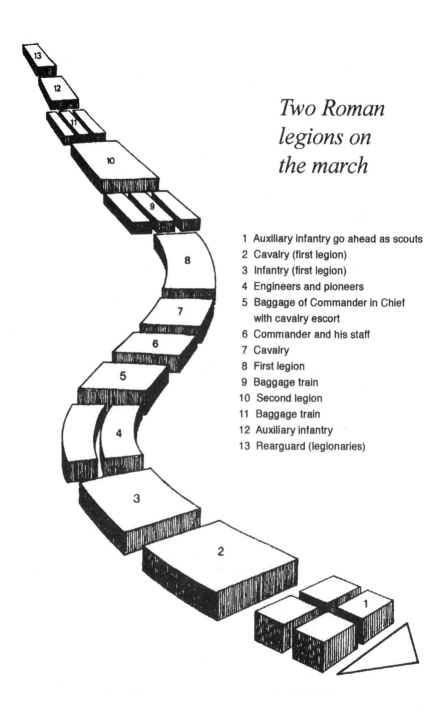

Two Roman legions on the march

1 Auxiliary infantry go ahead as scouts
2 Cavalry (first legion)
3 Infantry (first legion)
4 Engineers and pioneers
5 Baggage of Commander in Chief with cavalry escort
6 Commander and his staff
7 Cavalry
8 First legion
9 Baggage train
10 Second legion
11 Baggage train
12 Auxiliary infantry
13 Rearguard (legionaries)

MEDICUS   Doctor.

METATORES   Surveyors. See *agrimensor*.

MILIA PASSUM   Mile. The Roman mile was a thousand paces (1.4 kilometres).

MISSIO CAUSARIA   A term applied to a soldier who was invalided out.

MISSIO IGNOMINIOSA   Dishonourable discharge.

MODIUS   A metal container used as a dry-measure. See the famous one at Carvoran.

MUSCULI   Protective mantlets used by besiegers.

NUMERUS   An infantry unit drawn from the remote parts of the Roman Empire. They usually used their native weapons. There was a unit of bargemen from the Tigris at South Shields *(Numerus bareariorum Tigrisiensium)*. A similar cavalry unit was called a *cuneus*. There was a *cuneus Frisiorum*, a formation of Frisian cavalry, at Housesteads.

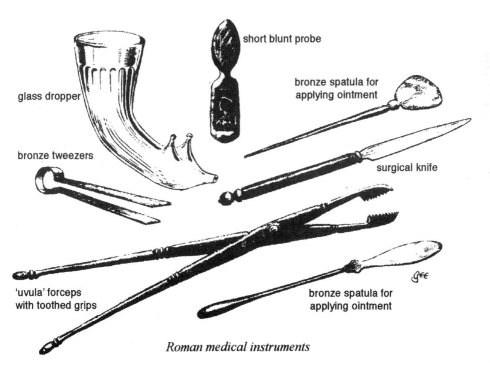

short blunt probe

bronze spatula for applying ointment

glass dropper

bronze tweezers

surgical knife

'uvula' forceps with toothed grips

bronze spatula for applying ointment

Roman medical instruments

IMP CA[ES]
SEVER [ALEX]
PIO [FEL. AVG. P. M.]
COS PP CVR
L[E]G AVG. [PR. PR.]
MP XIIII

Imperatori Caesari
Severo [Alexandro]
Pio [felici Augusto pontifici maximo]
consuli, patri patriae, curante
legato Augusti propraetore
millia passuum quatuordecim.

IMP CAES
FLAV VAL
CONSTANTINO
PIO AVG ET (?)
CAESARI
FL IVL
CONSTANTI
FIL AVG
· · E · LLO ·

Imperatori Caesari
Flavio Valerio
Constantino
pio Augusto et
Caesari
Flavio Julio
Constanti
filio Augusti
· · · ·

Roman milestones

24

OCREAE Greaves (armour for the protection of the legs). By late Republican times the only soldiers wearing greaves on active service were the centurions.

OFFICIUM The staff of a governor.

ONAGER The most powerful catapult used by the Roman army. It was named after the wild ass because of its kick.

OPPIDUM A Celtic stronghold usually on a hill top.

OPTIO The man beneath the centurion. His understudy. When he had been accepted for promotion to the centurionate and was waiting for a vacancy he was called *optio ad spem ordinis*. The officer in charge of a legionary hospital was called *optio valetudinarii*.

ORDO An early division of the legion.

PALUDAMENTUM The purple cloak of the commander-in-chief.

PAPILIO Tent made of leather.

PARMA EQUESTRIS The round cavalry shield used during the Republic.

PATERA Mess tin.

Roman skillet (patera) cast in bronze. Early 3rd century. Probably made in Gaul. Found in the wreck of a ship on the north sands at South Shields. Paterae were used for many purposes in Roman cookery, such as boiling stews and decocting wine, and sometimes had strainers. Each Roman soldier carried one.

Roman bridge at Corbridge (Northumberland)

PES pl. PEDES   Roman foot measuring 29.44 centimetres.

PECUARIUS   Soldier who attended farm animals.

PELTA   A small, light shield in the shape of a half-moon. Originally used by the Thracians and other barbarians.

PEREGRINI   Non-citizens. Applied to most of the inhabitants of Britain.

PERONES   Over-boots, worn by auxiliaries over their *caligae* in cold climates.

PHALERAE   Medal or discs worn by officers. They were decorated with heads of deities and worn on the chest.

PILA MURALIA   Stake for palisade.

PILUM   Spear. The heavy javelin of the legionaries.

PLUTEUS   A shed used by besiegers at base of walls.

PONS   Bridge.

PORTA   Gate. There were the following gates in a Roman fort - *porta decumana, porta praetoria, porta principalis sinistra and dextra. See Castra.*

PRAEFECTUS   Prefect. Commander of an auxiliary or allied battalion.

PRAEFECTUS CASTRORUM   The third in command of a legion. Camp prefect.

PRAEPOSITUS   Commander of a *numerus* or *cuneus*.

PRAESIDIA   A guard point.

PRAETENTURA   The front part of a camp occupied by the legionaries. The rear part *(retentura)* was occupied by lower units.

PRAETORIUM   Commanding officer's house.

PRANDIUM   Breakfast, one of the two meals for soldiers. See *Cena*.

PRINCEPS   Roman officer who was responsible for the headquarters staff of a legion and for training.

PRINCIPIA   Headquarters.

PTERUGES   Leather straps used on armour.

PUGIO   Dagger.

QUAESTOR   Quartermaster.

QUAETIONARIUS   Torturer or interrogator.

RETENTURA   See *Praetentura*.

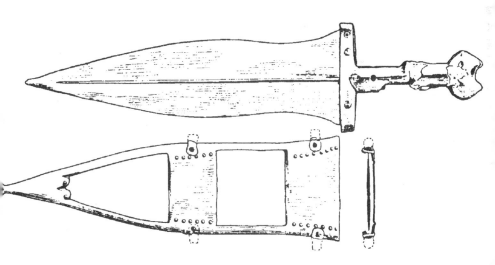

Large iron mounted dagger and sheath frame from Copthall Court, London, 3rd century.   *Museum of London*

Spatha

SACELLUM   Shrine of the standards. The central part of the *principia*. Beneath it was the strong room for keeping the unit's money and treasures.

SACRAMENTUM   Oath of loyalty taken by new recruits.

SAGITTARIUS   Archer.

SAGUM   Heavy cloak.

SCALAE   Scaling ladders.

SCHOLA   An officers' club.

SCORPIO   A small catapult.

SCUTATI   Troops bearing shields.

SCUTUM   A shield. The large curved legionary shield.

SESQUIPLICARIUS   Officer in an *ala*.

SIGNIFER   Standard bearer.

SPATHA   Auxiliary's long sword. Usually used by cavalry.

SPECULATORES   Originally a scout or spy. Later a messenger.

STELA   A pillar or column.

SUOVETAURILIA   The sacrifice of a ram, pig and bull for a *lustration* (purification).

TABERNA   Tavern.

TABULA ANSATA   Ornaments on neck guard of helmet with carrying handle.

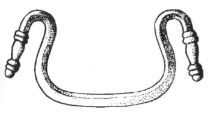

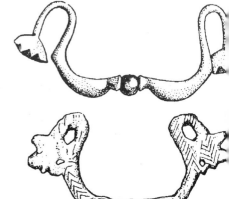

Carrying handles for helmets.

Corbridge and South Shields site museums

28

Chapel of an impressive headquarters building. A flight of stairs leads down to a sunken strong-room.

TESSERA   A small wooden plaque with the password written on it.

TESSERARIUS   The guard commander.

TESTUDO   Tortoise formation or an armoured siege machine.

TIBIA   A reed instrument. See *Aulos*.

TIRO   A recruit.

TITULUM   Short ditch in front of gate as a protection. See *Clavicula*.

TORMENTA   Artillery.

TORQUES   Neck bands - a military decoration.

TRIARII   See illustration below showing a *maniple of triarii* with 60 veteran spearmen and 40 *velites*.

TRIBUNUS   Senior officers who served under the legion commander.

TRIBUNUS ANGUSTICLAVIUS   Junior tribune.

TRIBUNUS LATICLAVIUS   Senior tribune.

TRIERARCH   Captain of a galley.

TROPAEUM   Trophy, memorial of a victory. A tree or pole from which the spoils were hung.

See triarii

30

Shield boss found at mouth of Tyne

TUBA Trumpet.
TUBICEN A trumpeter. The man who blew long-straight trumpets to signal the commander's orders.
TUBILUSTRIUM The feast of trumpets. A ceremony at which the musical instruments were purified twice a year on 23rd March and 23rd May.
TUNICA Tunic.
TURMA Cavalry unit of thirty horsemen.
UMBO Shield boss.

VALETUDINARIUM   A hospital.

VALLUM   An earthen wall or rampart set with palisades.

VELITES   Lightly armed legionaries.

VENATORES   Hunters.

VERUTUM   Javelin. Long thin spear.

VETERANUS   Veteran. Soldier who has completed his term of service or has re-enlisted.

VEXILLATIO   A detachment from one or more legions or auxiliary units selected for a special purpose.

VEXILLARIUS   The soldier who carried the Vexillum.

VEXILLUM   A cloth flag used as a standard especially for a cavalry *ala*. The only surviving example can be seen in the Museum of Fine Arts, Moscow. It was found in Egypt. The cloth is dyed red with an image in gold of a victory standing on a globe.

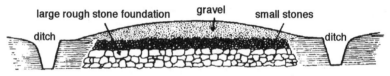

Cross section of a Roman road

VIA   A road.

VIA PRAETORIA   Road running from front to rear of camp.

VIA PRINCIPALIS   Road running from side to side of camp.

VIA QUINTANA   A secondary camp road running parallel to *via principalis*.

VICUS   Settlement of civilians living outside a fort.

VITIS   A centurion's emblem of office, a twisted vine-stick.